jus' sayn'

jus' sayn'

HELLER
LEVINSON

BLACK
WIDOW
PRESS

Boston

Joseph S. Phillips and Susan J. Wood, Ph.D., Publishers
www.blackwidowpress.com

Cover art: Linda Lynch, *Untitled Line Drawing,* oil on wood, 12 x 12 inches, 2021
Cover design: Linda Lynch
Layout: Kerrie Kemperman
Photo: Penina Meisels

ISBN-13: 978-1-7371603-7-3

Printed in the United States
10 9 8 7 6 5 4 3 2 1

for D.C. Wojiech who inspires & Heath Brougher who sustains

a manner a bid to spell out make sound swell forth
bring render tribute state exegete hyperbole has dimension
declensions level bevel off uneven fortitudes foothold gather this
is uneven sloppy often incoherent rambly disconnected humani-
tarian gestures welcome holy pilgrimages sought for this is gangly
disastrous this is an esSeizure an epileptic essay contorted torque-
twisting nefarious the subject is ONE DOWN, ONE UP
COLTRANE LIVE at the HALF NOTE Coltrane ever live
ever *say*'n to be Trane is to be the being of being Heidegger says
'the essence of our human being is that we exist within being'
where does being exist? at the Half Note being bees buzzbaroom
holy-roller holiday Friday March 26, 1965, 289 Hudson Street,
under the sign of Aries, people in the street listening to 'Stop! in
the Name of Love' by the Supremes, WABC hosting live for their
Friday nights 'Portraits in Jazz,' Mike Canterino (Half Note
founder) goes into kitchen asks his pop (the cook)where the veal
parmesan sandwiches are he's got a table of five hungry, pop says,
'Ma fammi il favore!' four suits white shirts & ties stroll through
door eyes magnify mouths petrify to check out these musical
gangsters these watershed angel Giant Steppers McCoy stands
over the piano plinks an F# Elvin mounts his cymbals Jimmy

picks up his bass & Trane stares at his Selmer Mark V1 sax
haunched on stand he's still like hummingbird he communes he
approaches his instrument as though it's *L*ive one word & you
expect the sax to leap into his hands love lavish licks ravish tone
holes bellows blow lunge longitudinal the 'say' in transmission on
the way   instruments = personalities   bruises dents badge of
honor scars character memory?   instruments solo, players
leave the stage, audience attunes to instruments, go to stage to
touch/fondle/embrace/peer question wood of the bass, the
history of the Gretsch drum, the roots of the Selmer company,
who tunes the piano, how often is it tuned, is the piano tuner
here tonight? is the soundboard Sitka spruce? Japanese spruce?
what's on tap ketchup with fries Trane exchanges chuckles with
Pops the players leave kitchen for stage to make musical history

>   *: tinder timber*

>   *chase tumbleweed go arch buddy blow*

>   *your heart out . . . .*

tenderly (Ben Webster 'tenderly') Trane reaches for his sax, the
arc of his bend blends with the ar(k)(ch) of his Mark V1, his
fingers flicker the keys, keypads adjusted just right, labia groom,

: when Trane replaced the
keypads he didn't use just any glue, he used
stick shellac because it hardens & won't
muffle the sound .....

fingers ://: keys → critical pressure to un-lid sound, scrutinized
precision, . . . lumbers to stage front, a small stage, barely large
enough for a quartet, sidles to mic, a commanding power
recalling the roots that reeled the sax to preeminence. . . :
April 1844, Adolphe Sax (his invention, his eponym) lusting for
success, saw an opportunity to inject his instrument into the
slack French military band which was eclipsed by the Polish/
Austrian competitors. Sax's Sax changed all that – the Sax-in-
fused bands triumphed over the competition & blazed the path
for the instrument's subsequent star power.

how much of

art

is

militancy?

Van Gogh: So much is demanded nowadays that painting seems like a campaign, a military campaign, a battle or a war.[1]

was military magnetism what drew militants to his performances?

The authentic artist, in addition to striving to import the vitalistic to somnambulistic surroundings, is committed to injecting freshness/new vigor into Art, necessitating a *break,* a 'downfall' of all that has preceded. Invention without repudiation.[2]

> : in 1914 the Vatican
> condemned both the turkey trot, the most
> popular dance, & the saxophone . . . .

Alan Grant introduces & announces: 'The John Coltrane Quartet ... as we broadcast the fine sounds of the Coltrane Quartet for the next 45 minutes or until midnight, of course this is the compliments of the people at the Half Note Club & the American Federation of musicians local 802, back to Jimmy Garrison:' *walk down broadway architectural laydown cylindrical*

---

[1] Letter 182, *The Letters of Van Gogh* (Penguin Classics).
[2] See *Wrack Lariat* (Black Widow Press, 2015) 179.

rotate bipedal carburet clunk cathedral 8th note crank Elvin lays down time on his 22 inch K-Zildjian riveted cymbal, Trane slips in, C# augmented over the A section, *crush systole carom cauliflower chorl call/response wail awhile*

> : One down, One up,
> the longest Coltrane
> solo ever recorded →
>
> 27 minutes 39 seconds

fuser hurl ore burst clay carom trollop chart jive dive wrap'round bound sound from soft shoe to the hucklebuck pluck cut-up raprout runrun riverran conical brass timbre trills multiphonic microtones groan moan freight train layin' twine quite like turpentine turkey trot bunny hop the kangaroo the shimmeshawobble burn kabob Janissary pedal peal

kahoot kaloot coalesce armature this pop parallelogram post bebop panoply broadcaster crowd-pleaser furl fallopian rollers tubes rods rambunction trill undulate splash thick vibrato honks squeals squalor banks enJEWELing

John-Edward Kelly:
If it doesn't sing and in some way dance, it isn't music.

grind smear bend pupate lactate delicate dictate sense sensate
sensorial scrotum tutorial

Jackson Pollock painted ONE while listening (at high volume) to the Count Basie band with Lester Young playing 'Jumpin at the Woodside' (the Decca side, 1938). It could be argued that ONE is a visual translation of Lester's lines.

How would ONE appear if Pollock had been listening to Coltrane instead? Would he have been so overwhelmed his brush hand would freeze? Or would his lines have morphed into monstrous frenetic slashes, more Franz Klein then the Prez-influenced-Pollock of ONE.

Could Beckett have written *Endgame* if he had been exposed to 27 minutes & 39 seconds of Trane? Hamm & Clov flopping about in ashbins? I mean, really.

C.D. Wright's 'Questionnaire in January:'
James Hillman said, Get out of history, get into geography. What
do you say?

I say: Get out of history, get out of geography, get into Jazz.

Dear John,
How many years has it been? I must have been 13 or 14, . . .
if our initiation was 'Kind of Blue' then it would be 14, but if
'Milestones,' then 13 years of age. An over 60 year relationship,
certainly one of my most enduring.

Back then: it was you, Miles, Blakey, Chico Hamilton, Gabor
Zsabo, MJQ, Dizzy, Ezra Pound, Gregory Corso, Rothko, Klein,
Joyce, Pollock, Der Blaue Reiter, Franz Marc, horses, Kafka,
playboy magazine, Hesse, Edgar Varese, . . . yeah, sure, so many,
buoys, flotation systems, the reason I didn't throw myself in front
of a train, Bertrand Russel, *re* having contemplated suicide at
sixteen: 'I did not however commit suicide, because I wished to
know more about mathematics.'

I read how deeply your father's death affected you. How you
were, what? 13? & suddenly bereft, . . .

The Coltrane biographer, Lewis Porter, writes:
Perhaps in a sense, music became his father substitute. And through music, he could both express and relieve the pain he felt about his father's death, a pain that he never seems to have allowed himself to fully explore.

you: mourning loss
me: inheriting parents I was averse to, mourning the absence of loss, . . . unable to access the feelings of loss that rent you so.

Clytemnestra pork chop tumbleweed short stop mitt oil bat rubber
cast the slide slip the jibber gauze feather graze pappappoppopcuddle
samblind day trade run fade heyday wry
convolute cahoot caboot carbuncle glide the long slow cattle slide
take outa hide stride blindside scalar exotic erotic D melodic-
harmonic minor slip ashore

Heraclitus:
The hidden harmony is better than the obvious.

On a saxophone the Reed is the vibrating substance. The most important factor in selecting a reed is the reed's thickness.

The reed is made of the cane plant. The cane has a hollow stem and grows to full height in one year. To make a reed, cane is cut to the proper length, cut along the length into four parts, and then shaved. Because reeds are made from a natural material, no two reeds are exactly the same.

Most of the cane for reeds is grown in the Var region of France. The *roseau,* or rushes, used for the reed are considered weeds that grow to about twenty feet. For years producers have tried to cultivate the plant but have found that only the wild variety produces a quality reed. The regions reed carvers believe an ancient spirit resides amid the *roseau:* when the wind blows, its singing can be heard all through the Var.

It seems fitting that the Half Note should have some reed plants growing around the room, arching & aching to the Trane sound, when the door opens, & the early Spring winds wind through, will the rushes sing, . . . singe?

I envision a young Trane, traipsing off to France to fashion his own reeds, deliberating & communing with the various plants before choosing, ardent evaluations, finally sizing up the chosen, talking to it, fondling, scrupulously shaving, crafting, organism to organism, . . . back in NYC, on stage, this fusion spirits through to audience, Trane's whole body, embouchure, hands fingers feet from the soil of the Var to a small downtown NYC stage, the human heart & the vegetal twined to dispatch . . . . *reed contagion arch persuasion till mill congregate expiate*

> : bass pedal;
> backbone of the kit; tempo
> scaffold; pulse mentor; guide
> star; ballast; bank; . . . .

sans bass kick drum nullity Be Bold bubble shoo fly ground terrestrial tight set sight like kite float bee superfly loft languor lush blush bur-geon hushly ....

The bass drum pedal was invented in 1909 by William Ludwig & was largely responsible for shaping the modern drum kit (America's only original instrument). The modern drumkit (that would mean 4 to 5 shells, or more, plus cymbals), developed from an Economic Need. Rather than paying multiple players — whereby one person would play the cymbals, one the bass drum, one the snare, etc., it could be reduced to the frugality of having to finance only one individual.

Is One Down, One Up satisfactory proof of an external world?

Does it follow the shadow of Dialectical Materialism?

puck muck luck dive jive drive tuck truck circumscribe describe
amortize play the fiddle go diddlediddleda-dum ka-rum

Were colonoscopies common practice in 1965?

Who won the world series in 1965?

bass pedal: bass-less → baseless → = unsupported, before Kenneth
Clark the bass drum was the official timekeeper, the boom
thwack. Kenny changed all that by syncopating the bass &
shifting time to the ride cymbal.

The baseline is paramount in sports.

He's off base

What do you base that on?

Bass-less with Elvin is immaterial, he is in no way hampered by
occluding a bass drum pedal.
Immateriality is Spirituality's sine qua non.

SUN SHIP JOHN COLTRANE 5> Ascent 10:10
Paul Chambers tread angelic, scrub steady, ladderly
'sun ship' recorded August 26, 1965, you can hear spillage from
ONE DOWN, ONE UP (hereafter abbreviated ODOU)
throughout these pieces. Check out the other 4 titles: 1> Sun
Ship; 2> Dearly Beloved; 3> Amen; 4> Attaining 'Attaining'
indicates where all the pieces are headed auguring with ODOU,
→ to the title of the 5th track, to → ASCENT!

how much of
ascent
is
increasing availability

In a mouthpiece, the turbulence caused by air passing over a reed
is noise.

Finding your own sound on the saxophone depends largely on
finding your personal combination of mouthpiece and reed.

Mouth the piece to say that says   speaks true who speaks shadows
shadow Sha-na na, Sha-na na na na na   scale calligraphy solar
soar   Most of the great jazz performances & recordings were un-
visited by sunlight. Played in the cave of bar, nightclub, in Rudy
Van Gelder's recording studio in Englewood Cliffs, New Jersey.

how much of
sunlessness
is responsible
for Sonic Soar

how much of
jazz
is a
solar appeal

ODOU, cat ballou *tube-tunnel trot lop lob lobby Parsifal*
precipitate participate threshold thrall intensity vortex lollapalooza
stash crash rash highroller

ROTTERDAM
Belize   Alca-
Pulco

Bertrand Russel showed that Descartes's brainstorm – 'I think
therefore I am' (a slogan which Descartes felt restored 500 years'
worth of neurotic intellectuals doubting their existence)– was
bogus. As Russel points out, the truth of 'I think' only proves the
existence of thinking.

Art Tatum plays 'Tiger Rag'

Had Descartes experienced ODOU would he become more doubtful? less doubtful? would the quality & quantity of his doubts alter? would he doubt that he was listening to music?

The Los Angeles Dodgers won the 1965 World Series.

Wayne Shorter:
The truth doesn't mean anything unless it has value.

         : what is the difference between
     heroin, alcohol, & god? is it that god is trans-
somatic? But it is said 'belief' can effect soma, can
even heal you.

trough scoop triplet splash paradiddlediddle coil rebound centrifuge
Aesop's Fables   Gypsy Rose Lee   Valentine's Day
   c i r c u m f l e x i o n

ElvTrane: the Parmenidean ineffable 'One' now Effable, . . .
playin', sayin', *loll meander hemoglobin cipher refoliate*
trans-discursive fuse ....

Hegel:
To be the negative of a nothing constitutes being. Being only *is* as
the movement of nothing to nothing, as such it is essence . . .
pure negativity, outside of which there is nothing for it to negate
but which negates only its own negative, and this negative, which
latter is only in this negating.

Pessoa:
And so I prefer the nothing of being nothing but that nothing.

Something, then, is that nothing which achieves its status by
virtue of negating. Nothing spurls through the ether by scraping
away *nots*. breath replaces breath, note, . . . note. cancellation
hopping the oscillate transpires, the vacuum of abyss surges.
undulation hatch   deep respiration   rural life   rum &
border collies

Heller:
There is neither something nor nothing.
Only *Shimmer.*

where in the upsurge

is

void

how much of

void

is

hearable

how do we know what another is hearing? could someone hearing ODOU be hearing what someone else is hearing when they hear Beethoven's ninth? Is that possible? How can we verify? By watching their feet? their bodily movements? Are we drifting toward the philosophy department?

infra-intra-ultrapolational migrate   nuclear opera   outlaws
outlayers   outliers   outfielders   meter–void technicality
succumb technology aplomb

Earl Bostic (1913 – 1965) introduced Coltrane to circular breathing.
Circulation as a vital element of organismic participation cannot be overemphasized.

In 1965 Lyndon B. Johnson was the American president.
Viet Nam: stagnation. Administration: stagnation. Logical Positivism: stagnation. Marriage: stagnation. The two party system: stagnation. Capitalism: _____ ? to be resumed

Cymbals are circular. Cymbals are the thinnest of instruments. Elvin played K-Zildjians at this time: 14 inch hi-hats, 18 inch crash, & a 22 inch riveted ride. In the 50's, Gretsch was the sole U.S. distributor for K-Zildjian when the Gretsch factory was in Brooklyn, NY (now located in Ridgeland, South Carolina where it produces the USA Custom, Broadcaster, & Brooklyn series). Folks at the factory recall Elvin coming down & spending the whole day playing cymbal after cymbal, meticulously evaluating, discerning, . . . listening.

During the intense ElvTrane entanglement, what are McCoy & Chambers thinking? are they digging the arpeggiated chords, the enharmonics, the intercourse of sax & cymbal splash, the pulsa-tile ascent splurge? Or perhaps they're pleased to have a break, wondering what they'll be having for dinner, how much monies from the gig will go toward rent, will they have sex tonight?

Paul: I need to change my strings
McCoy: The keys are sticky

where do birds go to die? does a bird ever expire in mid-flight? drop dead from the sky? of natural causes.

who was pitching for the Dodgers in the 1965 World Series?

Trane as pitcher ://: Elvin, Catcher

Can a scale run resemble a fastball?
A Blakey press roll?

Why compare anything to baseball?
Why compare at all? Doesn't that injustice the compared?

Comparisons strive to clarify. To supply additional contour to the compared.

Perhaps comparing drives us further away rather than closer to the compared.

It could be argued that comparisons serve to fortify connections that otherwise go unnoticed, . . . glittering the world with cosmic sparkle.

Where would literature be without comparisons?

Does music make comparisons? Comparisons differ from tunes being played differently. *mining the octatonic mirror on the wall hallball enthrall salute kaput salutary seize downward run runaway chromatic flurry furious famously*

CYMBALOLOGY: The first gallery exhibit consisting solely of cymbals. Cymbals from all around the world. Sabian Meinl Wuhan Zildjean Istanbul Agop, all shapes & sizes *circumlocunavihabitational sound   resound bound round sound pound down clown sound*

Samba sound Rock Mambo Hip Hop   Night in Tunisia sound

cymbal hilarity cymbal celerity cymbal circularity

sizzle cymbal hi-hat slap crash concede collide

cymbal singularity

singularly cordial-conviviALity

Capitalism plunders. is ethics void. subordinates to a single goal, → Profit. it don't matter how you get there. but get there you must to survive. CEO's answer to a board which answers to the shareholders which has one requirement = Profitability.

The modern day colonoscopy was first performed in 1969.

Sleeping with a guitar or violin seems more compatible than sleeping with a cymbal.
wood versus copper?

Where in the C minor wail is the Vietnamese child?

Wayne Shorter recalls:
Coltrane's experimentation was not only on the saxophone.
He would talk about his desire to speak the English language
backwards, to get at something else. To break patterns, I guess.
It was that innovative spirit that he had.

CYMBALOLOGY: in psalm 150, David exhorts 'Praise him
upon the loud cymbals; praise him upon the sounding cymbals.'
   Janissary holler rouse fire spitting armies animadversion
terreplein whop trebuchet trench counterweight sour saga rag
   Afro Blue Sound Love Supreme Sound   Kulu Sé Mama

Planetary Solution: Close down the fashion business & the phi-
losophy business & afford those workers a livable salary to restore
the planet.

Fashion: Do we really need to expend energies seeking out the
right color red this season? where the hemline should be?
Solution: Clothe the globe in suitable clothing for the region in
two colorways. Don't worry if WalMart is in town. Worry about
the ice caps melting, species extinctions, the rain forest.

Philosophy: Departments of philosophy, tenure, publish or
perish, 700 years proving/disproving, refuting/contrafuting the
existence of the external world.

Really?

This is not an anti-intellectual diatribe. Philosophy is a highly worthwhile endeavor. But not as a profession. Not to get paid for thinking. As Marx envisioned, philosophy would be done after the evening's meal, after the day's work was done, as a pursuit, not an occupation.

Wager: You harness all the urgent energy enumerated above & apply it toward solving our planetary concerns & bingo, — you'd have a recovering planet in under a year.

Perplexity is the bloom of thought.

Miles Davis loathed people who were comfortable.

Jack Kerouac:
The only people for me are the mad ones, the ones who are mad to live, mad to talk, mad to be saved, desirous of everything at the same time, the ones who never yawn or say a commonplace thing, but burn, burn, burn, ...

Dustin J. Hoffman gravitated toward those barely holding on, scratching to survive, bad credit risks, wrecks in their personal as well as their business lives.

                              : cymbals came into
          prominence during the Ottoman Empire when the
          Janissaries – the Sultan's elite fighting forces – clanged
          upon them before giving battle . . . .

the cymbal & sax both uprising from military contexts raises the question of whether TraneElv are locked in duel or embrace.
skit scatter score triumvirate wave dark matter   *umbrellas*
     dinosaurs

                    tan   ger   ine

Early 1959, Coltrane was becoming more intent upon forming his own group. It would be a tough decision to make as it would mean giving up the financial security afforded by the Miles Davis band.

In America, entrepreneurship has rock star status. 'Be Your Own Man' has become a mantra for self-respect. What does it mean to be your own man? Does it mean to 'own' oneself instead of being 'owned' by another. What does 'owning' mean? imply? Often

there is more personal freedom when the commercial require-
ments embedded in the term 'own' are handled by another so
that one is free from spending one's time on banal pragmatics.
On the other hand, Trane would have artistic freedom & thar's
the rub. Trane's sound was beginning to clash with the laid-back
cool brewing in the Miles mystique. Some eminent critics were
giving him a hard time: (*Down Beat,* August 22, 1957, p.32)
Kenneth Tynan describes his playing as 'superficially stimulating,
lonely, & rather pathetic self-seeking.'

burst	*flame to venture*	*to*	*Un-*
install	*Futur-fit*		
éclat	*curate*		*ConQuistador*

Tynan went on to call Trane's solos: 'overtones of neurotic
compulsion & contempt for the audience' (*Down Beat,* April 14,
1969, p.42).

Adding to Trane's craw was seeing Sonny Rollins gathering
acclaim since he'd left Davis. When Coltrane had played with the
Monk quartet at a special engagement, although his name was
listed, the ads boasted: 'Introducing in concert the Brilliant

Sonny Rollins.' What's more, in *Down Beat*'s critic's poll August 22, 1957, he was ranked #2 behind Sonny Rollins in the new tenor saxophone talent category.

Ratings, rankings, polls, hierarchical confabulations & the like are destructive manipulations. Music is not a competitive sport. Simply put, Bird   Dolphy   Trane   Cannonball   Webster   Brownie (among others too numerous to name) are All Great.

Comments like '___ was the greatest drummer who ever lived,' 'the best writer of his generation,' are all univocal myopic amputations. They shrivellize the world's richnesses, ... They are cheap capitalist maneuvers designed to enwrap product for ready consumption. Van Gogh   Cezanne   Picasso   De Kooning   Giacometti   Rothko   Monet   Pollock – All magnificent maestros. But no, we have to categorize, hierarchize, compartmentalize, linear-rate, — tame these monstrosities for convenient purchase, for easy digestion. Cultural packaging forestalls the generative swirl, suffocates the pulsative.

Ghettoizing minds is a further effect of this degradation. Supposing a newcomer to jazz sees his favorite sax player is ranked #23, he may begin to suspect his judgement, feel unschooled, inadequate, & might abandon his current inclination to follow the herd, to fit in, begin supporting the #1 pick instead. These foreshortenings, these breaches, penalize the gifts of Vastness.

Fernando Pessoa:
Let's not leave out a single god! [...] Let's be everything in every way possible, for there can be no truth when something is lacking! Let's create Superior Paganism, Supreme Polytheism! In the eternal lie of all the gods, the only truth is in all the gods together.

*swarm jag throttle multiplicitous beehive rake ragout   how are you
ya'hooo   who are you   do you do you   do do do do
dose do   heel/ toe   round & round   dose do*
third-related chords   Slonimsky ditone

Poetry/Dance = the most intrinsic of the arts. Music, sculpture, the visual arts, all require extra-somatic materials. Musicians bed in the lyre of instrumentation. The relationship a musician has with his instrument can not be overstated. Many concert pianists when contracting for tour insist on playing a Steinway piano & only a Steinway at each & every venue. Stevie Ray Vaughn slept with his guitar. Gene Krupa was buried with his snare drum (this has not been verified).

Jean Paul Sartre & Simone de Beauvoir were buried together in Le Cimitiere de Montparnasse. Insuring Eternal bone-bickering. Better to be buried with a violin then a mate. Avoid a death-time of aggravation.

When a musician is intimate with their instrument, it is no longer a property, a thing, but is now a treasure, a companion, a part of them. They may have named their guitar – as B.B. King did – Lucille. They know her moods, how she reacts to humidity, how to care for her when the atmosphere is overly dry or moist. They enjoy changing the strings, applying polish, . . . in short, they have as profound a relationship with their guitar as they do with their partner.
Lucille is infested with spirits, with magic, with animism.

Trane always had 9 or so mouthpieces in his dressing room. Constantly searching for the optimum setup. In the middle of a gig in Midtown NY, unhappy with his sax sound, he took a taxi to New Jersey to grab one more suitable.

Relentless searching for perfection.

Love arrived streaming jewels & sex appeal. a yellow ribbon. yards of ribbon. table of two. took a table for two. notes bend & waive, wave & dally, froth &flicker, ... freckles ... dither drivel, dream stuff, architecture & warm weather, woolies & teddy bears, ...

> how much of
> love
> is
> convention
>
> enterprise?
> conciliation?

Love loved martinis & olives. smelled 'olive' on the sax's breath.

1965 the Free Love Generation, plenty of sex, herpes, HIV, battle scars, tie-dye, no underwear. The generation that spawned the love generation were getting divorced in droves. If getting laid wasn't a problem, what fun is marriage?

Mudcat Grant, the pitcher for the Dodgers that won the world series in 1965, was being taken to the cleaners by his wife for his cheating ways.

In his defense, he said: 'But your honor, they're giving it away.'

In 1964, Trane called Naima, his first wife, to tell her that 90% of his playing would be prayer.

> how much of
> prayer
> is
> love

is prayer prayer without love?

is prayer love unceasing?

to attain the state of Love is heartbreak necessary?

heartbreak: strew pieces, smithereens, shards, rapture rupture, love kernels, injured, hurt . . . But alive, wriggling . . . battered, worn, shrunk fizzling jeopardized . . . But starch, emotionalgob-throbs unseemly indisposed pant pontoon buoyancy stretch grab a hold fertilizer betwixt between de-val-u-**a**-tion deny surge forward from foot sole to stellar soliloquy 'the heart has its reasons that reason does not know' Ozymandias king of kings its over when its over rollout meanwhile →

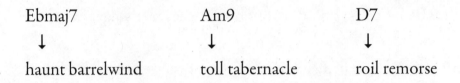

Ebmaj7   Am9   D7

↓   ↓   ↓

haunt barrelwind   toll tabernacle   roil remorse

By the time Trane formed his own group he was squeaky clean. His addictive personality confined his attentions two-fold: Music & butterscotch lifesavers.

How does addiction differ from obsession? is there a difference?

Could we say that addiction is bodily orchestrated while obsession is advanced inclination?

So that John Coltrane would be obsessed with music & addicted to butterscotch lifesavers.

Dear John,
There is much that I envy (perhaps 'envy' isn't the right word? covet?) about you. We've mentioned your love for your parents. Your capacity to feel loss & pain when they died. To know *mourning.*

& your love of god, your 'Love Supreme:'

'His way . . . it is so lovely . . .it is gracious. It is merciful – Thank
you God . . . . He is gracious and merciful . . .Thank you God . . . .
He is gracious and merciful . . . Thank you God. Glory to God . . .
God is so alive. God is. God loves.'

Your adamantine Belief boggles. Your pure conviction. Devotion.
Your innocence? purity? The god I know is a fireball, a thunder-
crack, an administrator of injustice, inequality, rancor, &
disregard. Simply a cock struttin piss strewin son of a bitch.

While you are fueled by your emotional surpluses, I am spurred
by my deficits, . . . my vacancies.

Trilogic Syllable
Mozart/Trane/Half-Note/Vienna – listening to Kristian
Bezvidentout playing Mozart's C major sonata, K.330 (c. 1782)
on fortepiano (Keyboard Tuning & Maintenance: Sion Neal)
recorded 2009, *peel moan sweep vista rally steeps/lows Trane*
spectrals fuses with fuselage canister ferry loam lumps sonic stretch
vascular hemoglobin gobfest Mozart/Trane Half Note/Vienna
hamburger/sachertorte 1782/2009 *division pierce bifurcation*
sanitize tally tuck wind wend thistle lather

Imagining Kristian Bezvidentout at the Half Note:
McCoy waves the 'Kid from Vienna' to the bandstand & moves
from the piano. Trane, wrapped in a private fury merely turns his
head. It was not possible to inject any more heat into the music.
To take it to another level.

But it happens: → Like some frenetic wildly erratic shooting star
Mozart flames fire. Flares flotillas of incendiary bolts –
rapier rattle   *strick bombast*
copious compound convulse abyss surge   Torrential
          Herculean

Covering the Unsaid with sound. To eke out, to lure from the
hidden, to *un*-conceal, to give speech to the unspeakable, to the
void that swells.

'It takes me that long to say what I got to say,' Trane responded
when Miles asked him 'why you got to play that long?'

And when Trane said, 'I just don't know how to stop,' Miles
replied: 'Try taking the horn out of your mouth.'

To motion the unsung – *lotion / emotion / devotion* → Trane
has been described as 'a mind in constant meditation.'

How do silence & the unspoken differ?
the unspoken doesn't speak. but silence speaks. often silence is
louder than speech.

THE EXPRESSED EXPRESSES THE INABILITY TO STATE WHAT IS SAID IN THE UNSAID

percolative vacuity
abyss smother
a surrender inconsistent with compromise

there is birdsong & primal scream
& the rock that sounds rivers
that coaxes

a hearing present

TRANSLITERATING TRANE TRANLITERATING MORANDI

David Zwirner Gallery 20th Street Tuesday, March 16, 2021, 10:32 am.

In front of a Morandi oil painting: 6 upright objects — 3 bottles/1 vase/1 pitcher/& a yellow rectangle — all about 6 inches tall except for the yellow which stands about 2 inches: growing into the painting, birthing occupancy, reeling-in, casting-in, . . . dominant motifs → Intimacy/Cheer/Repose = this is what Community looks like, hard to move away, such good company, such good conversation, these objects deviate from Object-hood, become neighborhood, . . . I imagine Coltrane in front of the painting, holding his soprano sax, transfixed, . . . would he find a key for the painting? would he change keys after a few measures? what notes would he transpose the yellow with, the blue, the ebony, the ivory? what words enliven the colors, extend, enrich them? does he hear chords? is Morandi modal? Trane brings the sax to his mouth, limbers his fingers, his eyes don't leave the painting, he plays: *golden bicycle wind river rend beaver hustle quartet colloquy proud pastures green animals dandelion grasshopper   glide   slide   sideslip   rock gardens   emerald molten*

                    moccasin

                    moss

starlight   *fugues*   *Ravel*

                         butterscotch

John Locke says Wisdom is the 'science of happiness.'

Trane counters with: Wisdom is the 'science of saxophone.'

Happiness as the holy grail runs rampant. from the Greek
Eudaimonia (the harmonious operation of the elements, . . .
flourishment) to the Enlightenment & onto the American
constitution to everyday life 'happiness' reigns as the over-
arching ideal.

Artists are not happiness consumers. They are committed to sayn'
it, gettin' it out, gettin' it right. 'One Down, One Up,' isn't
happiness, — it is otherly, transmutative, transformative, eerily
ethereal, cheerily ecstatic, frighteningly bold, loaded wih blister.

Nietzsche opposed the popular view that happiness should be
our guide to ethical behavior.

Thus Spoke Zarathustra:
Do I strive after happiness? [No,] I strive after my works!

Twilight of the Idols:
Man [should] not strive after happiness.

For Nietzsche, for the artist, happiness is not a default, it is a by-product, the result of exertion, of Excoriate Exhale, . . . of Wrack Lariat.

Wrack: 'to undergo, ruin or subversion; to reject, refuse.

A means or cause of subversion, or downfall' (OED).

The term *Wrack Lariat* suggests the artist's mission. A mission compelled to reject all that is stale, handed down, — habituated. An Enterprise – in its commitment to the Vitally Essential – intolerant of falsehoods, of the trivially redundant, of the Uninspired Quotidian.

The Artist, wracked with subversive determination, hurls a lariat (extending *outward*), a hurl both tremulous & nervy, daring to loop the Wildly Original, The Never-Before-Seen, & lead it home, . . . undomesticated, yet found.

To reap Insight, massive exertion must be exercised, much con-
tortion. Rilke believed that difficulties serve to shape the artist.

In the fifth elegy, Rilke imagines the time when the acrobats were
still acquiring their skills, still developing, —

'oh where in the world is that place in my heart

where they still were far from being *able,*

[the 'able' here refers to the virtuoso's fluency, where the body is so well
trained it can go through its maneuvers mechanically, soulless, distanced
from the more real period of struggle where mind & body are assiduously
'earning their stripes,' where they]

Still fell away from each other like mounting animals, not yet

properly paired; —

where weights are still heavy,

and hoops still stagger'

where their endeavor had 'weight,' not 'the empty too-much.'
Proficiency without emotion is empty capability.

Seeing Rudolf Nureyev perform two sloppy pirouettes has more emotional impact than watching his colleagues perform five flawless pirouettes. Pirouettes soaked in vapidity.

Happiness   eye gouge groin slam carcinogenic radioactive viral vituperate macular degenerate vascular clot spiritual clog crud corrode testicular rot machete massacre territorial burn industrial toxicity — Happiness & the horse you rode in on — starvation stagnation degradation bullet riddle ocean foul iceberg melt polar bear skate away take away the 'take' mantra repeat after me   Happiness pursuit of   the right to equal degeneration stripped of   fraught with right to prosper   multiply mangle mingle barter slaughter tear down make room build to build prosper develop developer Happiness is developers developing
          the right to   with equal pleasure   develop prosper make miserable   decimate   rank rancid putrescent vapidity a failed species   take your Happiness & ____ __
In the ninth Elegy, Rilke asks:
'Are we, perhaps, here *just for saying* [italics mine]: House, Bridge, Fountain, Gate, Jug, Olive tree, Window,— possibly: Pillar, Tower? .... but for saying, remember, oh, for such saying as never the things themselves hoped so intensely to be. Is not the secret purpose

of this sly earth, in urging a pair of lovers,
just to make everything leap with ecstasy in them?

. . . .

Here is the time for the Tellable, *here* is its home.
Speak and proclaim.'

The 'say,' then, that ventures beyond speech as utensil, beyond the
bruise that pulls things apart, sucks the life out of them, to
replace this sunder with word as pure word fusing every-thing
with leaps of ecstatic epiphany.
To Robe the Cosmos in Revelation.

ODOU

First chorus B section *vibrato cumulative weight ponder Bmaj.
phrase Bmaj./G/Eflat augmented triad ripple rave current rash vast
vascular flush ascent immerse* disrupt *stasticity sclerotic leprosity*
inoculate *salty dog Hudson Street   Kansas City   New Orleans
Philadelphia   Birdland   Art Tatum   Bean   Diz/Bird/Roach
Prez   Brownie   Delilah   Basin Street   destination worship
trance saloons dhyana parlors Ceres succulent horns of grain reel
reek prayer meetin' caterwaul cakewalk gypsy Django slow juicy
tango heel toe dosy-do*

CADILLAC TO DROP TAIL FINS FOR '65

Tail fins were style with a purpose and the purpose was simple:
sell more cars.

The Number One Single in Billboard magazine's Year-End 100
songs of 1965 was:
"Wooly Bully" performed by Sam the Sham and the Pharaohs.

Uno dos, one two tres quatro

Ay, wooly bully
Watch it now, watch it

Here he comes, here he comes
Watch it now, he get 'cha

Matty told Hatty
About a thing she saw
Had two big horns
And a wooly jaw

Wooly bully
Wooly bully
Yeah drive
Wooly bully
Wooly bully
Wooly bully

Springin' the 'Say' that 'Says:'

If we are here *jus'* for saying & Coltrane is sayin' it & Van Gogh says it, Morandi says it, & Giacometti & Gustaf Sobin & a host of others say it, how does the sayin' get said?

Up front it must be declared that the following does Not say it. At best it will be an intimation, an approximation, a flawed & insufficient accounting:

Fundamentally, creativity oozes from the magical & to disentangle the magical would be to subvert the enterprise. But we have clues & tools.

We begin with former explorations of the Delve/Immerse-Into which employs 'Prolongation,' an extended marination to Sink/DelveImmerse-Into the subject/term one is addressing:

with
prolongation, ...   maneuver
irritability,   — complaint
.....
purloin quiddity loin launch mastication therapies altitudinous
gain no gainsay quibble
grit grainy to robust go

archaelology   the dig   uncovering
perturbation   pertination
present

A 'quick' take on the above application: to prolong is against the grain in our culture therefore one must 'maneuver' become 'irritable' with the blockages and of course rag (complain) about them ... then a ZAP, a Zinging Activation Procedure, (a long large mouth/lung full of a legato one breath fractally collusional line intended to de-stabilize & to evoke (not to claim) alterior reassemblies) which campaign to nutritionally gain altitude and steer toward the 'robust, the realm of loin and therapy, and what we are working with in this Hinge Application is an archaeology, digging into the logos, the word uncovering perhaps perturbing material yet 'pertinent,' ('pertination' = neologism) and then to present the results of our dig which is the application.

A prolonged concentration upon the Term enables a *Fusing-With,* a *Knotting.*

KNOT
intercoursing vocabularies ravel
revel protuberant   bundleclaspintertwine
bulb conversational cavort quid-
ity commingle   strand coalesce
quanta   parcel jam friction flare accumu-
late

gather-swell

The Sink/Delve/Immerse-Into is an essential component of the Gaze which is an essential component of 'sayn'.'

       where in the
       prolong
       is the
       still

Sayin' the Gaze:*

How does the gaze differ from the look, the peer, the regard, the delve-immerse/into, or what Van Gogh called "watching?" To give 'gaze' as wide a berth as possible, gaze will be viewed as inclusive of the above terms plus others that satisfy the criteria of any prolonged & intense seeing whose intention is to *peer-into* with an eye toward extraction.

What is it exactly that we are hoping to extract? It is the essential beingness of what is on view, its quintessential quiddity. The 'that' which is *before* one, which presents itself as *appearance*

The gaze, is flotational, disallocational, non-mechanistic, anti-sequential, non-transactional, attenuative, nuanced, & fluid — the gaze euphorizes to the rhythmic flux of Bergsonian duration.

Key interrelated components of the gaze are:
1. Suspension 2. Absence 3. the Peer

To mobilize the term to come forth, one must disengage oneself
from the temporal, one must 'stand still like the hummingbird.'
Just as human movement in the forest will cause animals to
scatter, so the model may be fragile & elusive, reluctant to appear
unless secure of a non-threatening & appreciative clearance.
The viewer must attain a state of suspension, must ready the
perceptual pores for complete receptivity. This state of complete
openness is achieved by *absenting* all considerations, banishing
all distractions, obstacles, & blockages. Perhaps most difficult
of all, the 'self' must dissolve, must melt into a reservoir of
communality, must *delve-immerse/into* the Other. When such
conditions apply, term will generate activity, will vibrate with
appeal, will become succulent with invitation. The unremitting
drift of additional magnetically accumulative phenomena in
differing articulations requires the gazer to keep peeling away
the facets to insure complementary densification.

The gaze is more than mere reception. Prolonged deep-seeing
releases the see(e)r & model from the situated as they fuse to a
current charged with shimmer, with diffuse & formulation, new

liveliness's spawn, unlikely shapes appear, the trans-retinal whorl-blends with the strictly perceptive, dimension oscillates, horizon flutters, optical fireworks bedizen.

This coupling, this interosculative *other*-ling, constitutes the *magni*-ficence of the gaze.
Less dialogue, than
con-gress.

* Much of the 'gaze' discussion above was borrowed from "Giacometti's Gaze," *Un-,* Black Widow Press, 2019.

Extraction Tools:

Churn: 'To agitate vigorously or turn over repeatedly.'

Turbulence or agitation: 'the violent churn of a long waterfall.' (American Heritage Dictionary).

Elements of Churn: drill, press, engage, render, — wrangle with, grab a bull by the horns, drill → to make a hole, penetrate, repetitious application,

crank   contort   torque,   twist   bore into, open, openings, . . . interosculate

constellate

fabricate

woodshed

Trane was constantly practicing, woodshedding,— when the band took a break he would go to the dressing room to practice rather than carouse — considering, never content, never willing to be comfortable with his music-making just because it was well received, always questing for more, for further, *churning* toward dev-el-op-ment, toward gettin' it, *sayin'it.*

When Neils Ertegun, co-founder of Atlantic Records, needed some additional incentive to nudge Coltrane to sign with Atlantic & leave Prestige Records, he offered a car of his choice as a signing bonus.

Trane chose a Lincoln Continental.

Miles's favorite car was a Ferrari Tesstarosa.

Miles was a fashion connoisseur.

Trane would wear the same boxy suit for a whole week.

Miles loved the women.

Trane love the saxophone.

jus' sayn'.

ODOU, 10:49 into the solo,

McCoy &
Jimmy back away, it's
jus' Trane & Elvin . . .

coiled into One Soil:
from one soil this coil
jus' Trane, & Elv', merged meshed mashed into one supreme
meritorious organism, → TraElve   TranElvin   ElvTrane
take the A train hydroplane bombinant bazaar Brooklyn's Club
La Marchal La Bamba Bop Bully burlesque harlequinade
smithereens smash circumstantial

: about 16 minutes into the solo
Elvin breaks his bass drum pedal, it's
only sticks, skins, cymbals . . . & Trane . . .

calliope curl caliper crunch unified undivide trench celestial
terraplane devil at the door angelic implore rat-a-tattat still got the
hi-hat bounce bop barrel flare fling turbo flung turbulent jump start
initiate granular gravitas gruel the stuff of dreams moreover clover
cereal sacrifice enchant the queen fertilize enterprise pass the gravy
stir

crazy . . .

Jimmy Heath while discussing his difficulties with playing modal tunes says "I wasn't the only one who had this problem. Coltrane, who was also playing modal compositions, had to decide on a good musical ending when he played in that style. One of the reasons Trane kept playing chorus after chorus was that, as he himself said, he 'could not find anything good to stop on.'"

The Butterfield Blues Band debut album was released by Electra Records in October 1965.

Love loved. what was not to love? ElvTrane in ecstatic soar, a dry martini, — what was not to love? Love was confused about love but now, now it was self-evident, it was there, on the bandstand in her ears eyes heart, ... it beamed, volute. people ask how she got her name she says her parents, no, she doesn't know what it means any more than Sally knows what Sally means, or Sarah, Bobby, or Mike. she knows love is a loaded word, it fans out – 'I love you/I love you too' – she's had relationships, she's had feelings, but not anything like this, what she feels now . . . her relationships seemed to proceed from skirmish to satisfaction, skirmish to satisfaction, . . . where was the elation? the loft?, . . . where the ekstasis she was experiencing here, right now, . . . this *swarm*.

SWARM
castoff percolate enormity heave-ho throw heft
                              Bora Bora
                    chicory cluck
drive wound thread ventricular helium slippage sensorial
spool velocity cascade uplift cocoon undulate spiral bound
oath air aria voice singular muscular meticulously
elaborate

Vintage Zildjian K's = the holy grail, lusted after by jazz drum-
mers for decades, commanding outrageous prices, — 'K' stands
for Kerope 11 who took control of the Zildjian Co. following the
death of his brother Avedis 11 in 1865. He introduced a line of
instruments called K Zildjian. *Elvin whack crash ride tarentalla*
pop slash plash Squall sunder testify Elvin Cymbal Samurai

In the 50's Gretsch were the drums of choice for such luminaries
as Elvin Jones, Tony Williams, Art Blakey, Philly Joe Jones,
Jimmy Cobb, Chico Hamilton, Mel Lewis & others. Since all the
above were Gretsch endorsers, it was convenient for them to
choose K's readily available at the Gretsch factory in Brooklyn.

K mania 2021: Nicholas Margarite, sole proprietor of Nicky Moon Cymbals, a one man operation in New Jersey, sends out an email:

Old World Unearthed
Buried Underground for 30 Days!

True old world craftsmanship combined with a real in-earth aging process to give you the ultimate vintage vibe. Been dreaming of an old stamp Istanbul K, . . . ? these are the first official Old World Unearthed cymbals by NickyMoon and are numbered #1, #2, #3, #4 and #5. Own a piece of modern cymbal history! https://www.instagram.com/tv/CNNPOV0glwX/?utm _source=ig_web_copy_link

Voila, the beat goes on. Imagine 19th century Istanbul cymbal makers hammering bronze all day by hand, imagine how they would marvel at the spectacle of K's unearthing from New Jersey on instagram!

Dear John,

Lost today. disconsolate. on desolation road.

the road to desolation road

  abject   scowl

scummed perturb rot reticulate

atrophic carcasses pave   wet gravid

sorry, John, I got carried away. if I had a saxophone I'd blow my
blues out. not away. but out. why do away with blues,
melancholy, tristesse? they sound so *gooood*. I'd take my sax, take
my gloom to the streets, slam my gloom before the people. court
audiences with misery. with the virtuosity of maudlin. not many
artists can do it. evoke deep pathos. in literature the Russians &
Europeans got it, — Dostoevsky, Tolstoy, Chekov, Nietzsche,
Kafka, Baudelaire, . . . scant pickings in America, maybe three:
Emily Dickinson, Melville, Faulkner. but you got it in spades,
John. perhaps it's easier with a horn, that brass just goes deep
inside the body, whisks the soul feathers (feathers the soul
strings), balloons feelings.

Maybe you don't get affected, maybe as soon as the gloom come your way it's ushered through your horn, it has no chance to bed inside you, to eat away, to chip to chafe, you use it, transform glum into notes, architecture, sound, work with it, toy, mold, then pro-ject, play . . . perform . . . .

Cioran writes: 'It is almost incredible how fear sticks to the flesh; it is glued there, inseparable from it & almost indistinguishable from it.'

Your saxophone = the non-stick surface.

how much of

innovation

is a

'stumble-upon'

case in point: bebop: it could be argued that bebop was inaugurated when Kenny Clark (known as 'Klook') fractured the conventional 4/4 beat. In his own words:

It just sort of happened *accidentally* [italics mine] . . . the tempo
was too fast to play four beats to the measure so I began to cut
the time up. But to keep the same time going, I had to do it with
my hand, because my foot just wouldn't do it. So I started doing
it with my foot, to kind of boot myself into it. . . . When it was
over, I said, 'Good God, was that ever hard.' So then I began to
think, and say, 'Well, you know, it worked. It worked and nobody
said anything, so it came out right. so that must be the way to do
it.' Because I think if I had been able to do it [the old way], it
would have been stiff. It wouldn't have worked.

Error as Avengement →
Drummer Hal Blaine's epochal moment was not so much
accident as mistake (which overlaps accidental). On the hit
record 'Be My Baby' by the Ronettes, he missed a beat in the
pattern &, in his words, 'being the faker that I am, anytime I
make a mistake, I will continue that mistake. . . That mistake was
one of the wildest things that ever happened to me to this day.'
This became the famous lick that every drummer in the world
was playing.

    originality ://: innovation

    experiment ://: invention

How to distinguish:
mistake/accident/originate/experiment/innovate/stumble-
upon/chance/luck/ creativity

The above terms overlap, bleed-through, co-configure &
compound. Any attempt to disentangle this consortium is
destined to spoil the bouillabaisse.

When Kenneth Clark attempts to accommodate the demanding
pace of 'Old Man River' by freeing-up his limbs from their
former assignations, he stumbles-upon & accidentally innovates
an original rhythmic complexion.

cradle pinwheel pancreatic prance stay a while smither ye bonkers
good soil is rich in nutrients wish you were here when it's over come
to a decision before matters deteriorate to the barely audible the
rarely seen seam pockets dust jackets overly populated barometric
confusion according to procedure
scantily clad but fulsome

When Hal Blaine creates a mistake by misreading the chart he
chances upon/originates a new lick that becomes world famous.

Where does accident leave off & innovation begin? luck &
invention? chance & originality? experiment & discovery?

how much of

genius

is

accidental

Today in my email.
Poet Interlocutor: Monsieur. ça va?

Heller: Yes, Dahlin', so very yes Yes, . . . am under Siege,
Besieged, words ripping me, dreams dreadlock my wake-eyes, I
who never write about/with the 'I' am drowning in I, an I that
sunders tears fathom freaks depths of despair (?) hunger (?)
'savage proposals' (?), I can no longer be institutionalized, I have
been labelled inadmissible, a 'danger' to others, I electrocute
electricity, fry their electroshocks, . . . is this self a self any longer
or an emission, a tsunami of pain torrential grief catastrophe — I
invite catastrophe/demolition/sanitizing destruction — can you
hear me? do I stutter? do I offend too much? am I still ugly?
would you change me? this me that spews excruciates, devil
dung, apple sauce — this is not a self this is a parody, a farce, a
diversion, the worst is yet to come
i fear it, it fears me,
i will tear it apart
it will tear me apart

why resist?

Poet: Unusual weather here but I love it: overcast for more than a week. What's the weather saying there?

Heller: I am Weather. I am cloud & fern tree, caterpillar & devil's milk. I 'I' too much, aye aye, I can't stand writers who use their I, who digest themselves like breakfast pills, who have no Other, I repudiate their trivialities, keep them away from me, do you hear, — away, a*Way* . . .
I rain, I joust, I make love with the sun, with moon, with nimbus & cumulus too, with brook, with bellies & thighs,
I surround Thunder with My Wet Lips!

Poet: The living are still haunting me. The dead give me comfort. How are your dead/living treating you?

Heller: from LESSNESS (*LURE,* Black Widow Press, 2022).
the ghost of the loved one lives larger than the loved one live.
track the
fade.   the vanish.   (vanquish?)
absence out-presences presence.

lessness is not strictly correlative.

lessness: the not nothing that is not much.

Oct. 29, 1965: Publication date of THE AUTOBIOGRAPHY OF MALCOLM X.

Malcolm writes:
Be peaceful, be courteous, obey the law, respect everyone, but if someone puts his hands on you, send him to the cemetery.

I'm having trouble, John, with the 'courteous' admonition. I mean, balls out, who gives a crap about 'being courteous.' the thing is to get it right & slam it home, slap the universe awake. no time for soft shoe pussy footin' 'correctness,' . . . .

Art is War. You have to slaughter everything that preceded you, you have to slaughter everything currently blocking your way, & you have to shock bomb the future with an original paradigm that fails to dislodge.

  trill tympanic thrombotic denounce   escalate equipage full frontal

if they come within striking distance for good measure upon hearing the news run for on the eve of impertinence if only it wasn't your solo a slippery tune play over

John, do you ever get so alone? i'm sure, But, you've got your
instrument. instrumentation. the full scale of instrumentation
has yet to be realized. whether brass wood wind animal skin bone
stick no matter. instruments are instrumental to human being.
musicians are especially wedded to their instruments. & why not,
— a sax won't up & leave you, a sax can hear your pain, absorb yr
pain, transform yr pain, from pinched excruciate reed reclaim
hallelujah blues in the belly of love in the Phrygian mists of
imaginal fructuosity, . . . did you have a name for your sax? i
would have a name for my instrument, i name everything, —
cars, pens, boulders, trees, all is animate burble pop cradle rock
lavender, ...

when all is said & done there's say. we're back to that. or start
to that. say said sing song sayn' song sayn' wind breeze
lunglungelonging, . . . hug
nocturnes   pathos ponds   syzygal gusts   dive bars

you can't simulate my alone, John. stranded sans instrument.
without.
sloughing through desolate sands.
scraped, soul-slithering . . .
. . singular.
. . stained.
. . stranded

STRANDED

scrape   minstrel scalped
misled bedlam bells noise fester 'apart' cadenced saprogenic gaps
accrue
suck-holes proliferate evangelical tidings hush
like a shutdown sea,
a final shorn,
across piteous belly swathes
nefarious wafts stone cold
dead in the market

disrupt,
pronounced rift muscular articulate alien, I join the bandstand,
hand me yr sax, ready-set-go, I up wind grind grin grandee, like
deer feet, like fodder, butterfly, grin gamely where's the beat to
my heat, combust collude, where's the ride cymbal, the bass, up
up away awry ajar take it far fling, rhythm section up & gone,
skidoodle, all is lost, no not lost, I'm groovin' blarin' not carin'
swearin' liposuction take me to the bank left aside with no ride
alone
outside
deride
beside

Night In Tunisia
with no ride

across barriers seas I scrape absentee absently absurd postures
jubilant teeth mongers rupture frost fire from furry things end of
the line I refuse to give up I go lion
sandals
surreption

John Coltrane's *MEDITATIONS* recorded November 23, 1965.
that'd be a Tuesday, not a date night. a little over six months since
ODOU. expurgate days of the week expurgate hours time
schedule catch tardy punctual weather bring an umbrella
ODOU spills transfuses floods MEDITATIONS *Trane-Helm*
the father & the son & the holy ghost helter skelter 2 tenors
(Trane & Pharaoh Sanders) 2 drumkits (Elvin & Rashied Ali)
multiphonic caravel cluster catalyst catalectic ruminate rhumba
outlier parodic complexity hanger screech honk holler maelstrom
relay rumble LOVE is the third track, nothing soupy smarmy
no treacly sweet but panperspectival the vast whole visionarial
panoply of Love, — ache, scorch, sweet, serenity, tumult, pain,
agony, ecstasy, bliss . . .
this is love

Love: filler that balloons space
    : the illusion that justifies

        how much of

        love

        is

        panic

there are those you left behind, from ODOU on, those who couldn't keep up, . . . you never feared losing your audience, you only feared the journey discontinuing, the search aborted, you, the archetypical *Wrack Lariat,* who strove to inflate *say* into an infinite immaculate *shiver . . .*

robust roundabout rill extravagant silver spur panther flare skew-bald prance I go mango I go thistle & tumbleweed Tonto & Madagascar trigger spun I go Vast Whetted Appetitive, I go whoopsy diddly doo paramount surmount, ether parade serenade, . . .

let's
go outside, John

BLACK WIDOW PRESS :: POETRY IN TRANSLATION

Approximate Man and Other Writings by Tristan Tzara. Translated and edited by Mary Ann Caws.

Art Poétique by Guillevic. Translated by Maureen Smith.

Beginnings of the Prose Poem. Edited by Mary Ann Caws, Michel Delville.

The Big Game by Benjamin Péret. Translated with an introduction by Marilyn Kallet.

Boris Vian Invents Boris Vian: A Boris Vian Reader. Edited and translated by Julia Older.

Capital of Pain by Paul Eluard. Translated by Mary Ann Caws, Patricia Terry, and Nancy Kline.

Chanson Dada: Selected Poems by Tristan Tzara. Translated with an introduction & essay by Lee Harwood.

Earthlight (Clair de Terre) by André Breton. Translated by Bill Zavatsky and Zack Rogow. (New & revised ed.)

Essential Poems and Prose of Jules Laforgue. Translated and edited by Patricia Terry.

Essential Poems and Writings of Joyce Mansour: A Bilingual Anthology. Translated with an introduction by Serge Gavronsky.

Essential Poems and Writings of Robert Desnos: A Bilingual Anthology. Edited with an introduction and essay by Mary Ann Caws.

EyeSeas (Les Ziaux) by Raymond Queneau. Translated with an introduction by Daniela Hurezanu and Stephen Kessler.

Fables in a Modern Key by Pierre Coran. Translated by Norman R. Shapiro. Full-color illustrations by Olga Pastuchiv.

Fables of Town & Country by Pierre Coran. Translated by Norman R. Shapiro. Full-color illustrations by Olga Pastuchiv.

A Flea the Size of Paris: The Old French Fatrasies & Fatras. Edited and translated by Ted Byrne and Donato Mancini.

Forbidden Pleasures: New Selected Poems 1924–1949 by Luis Cernuda. Translated by Stephen Kessler.

Furor and Mystery & Other Writings by René Char. Translated by Mary Ann Caws and Nancy Kline.

The Gentle Genius of Cécile Périn: Selected Poems (1906 –1956). Edited and translated by Norman R. Shapiro.

The Great Madness by Avigdor Hameiri. Translated and edited by Peter C. Appelbaum with an introduction by Dan Hecht.

Guarding the Air: Selected Poems of Gunnar Harding. Translated & edited by Roger Greenwald.

Howls & Growls: French Poems to Bark By. Translated by Norman R. Shapiro; illustrated by Olga K. Pastuchiv.

I Have Invented Nothing: Selected Poems by Jean-Pierre Rosnay. Translated by J. Kates.

In Praise of Sleep: Selected Poems of Lucian Blaga. Translated with an introduction by Andrei Codrescu.

The Inventor of Love & Other Writings by Gherasim Luca. Translated by Julian & Laura Semilian. Introduction by Andrei Codrescu. Essay by Petre Răileanu.

Jules Supervielle: Selected Prose and Poetry. Translated by Nancy Kline & Patricia Terry.

La Fontaine's Bawdy by Jean de La Fontaine. Translated with an introduction by Norman R. Shapiro.

Last Love Poems of Paul Eluard. Translated with an introduction by Marilyn Kallet.

A Life of Poems, Poems of a Life by Anna de Noailles. Edited and translated by Norman R. Shapiro. Introduction by Catherine Perry.

Love, Poetry (L'amour la poésie) by Paul Eluard. Translated with an essay by Stuart Kendall.

Of Human Carnage—Odessa 1918–1920 by Avigdor Hameiri. Translated and edited by Peter C. Appelbaum with an introduction by Dan Hecht.

Pierre Reverdy: Poems, Early to Late. Translated by Mary Ann Caws and Patricia Terry.

Poems of André Breton: A Bilingual Anthology. Translated with essays by Jean-Pierre Cauvin and Mary Ann Caws.

Poems of A.O. Barnabooth by Valery Larbaud. Translated by Ron Padgett and Bill Zavatsky.

Poems of Consummation by Vicente Aleixandre. Translated by Stephen Kessler.

Préversities: A Jacques Prévert Sampler. Translated and edited by Norman R. Shapiro.

RhymAmusings (AmuseRimes) by Pierre Coran. Translated by Norman R. Shapiro.

The Sea and Other Poems by Guillevic. Translated by Patricia Terry. Introduction by Monique Chefdor.

Sixty Years: Selected Poems 1957–2017 by Mikhail Yeryomin. Translated by J. Kates.

Through Naked Branches by Tarjei Vesaas. Translated, edited, and introduced by Roger Greenwald.

To Speak, to Tell You? Poems by Sabine Sicaud. Translated by Norman R. Shapiro. Introduction and notes by Odile Ayral-Clause.

BLACK WIDOW PRESS :: MODERN POETRY SERIES

WILLIS BARNSTONE
ABC of Translation
African Bestiary (Forthcoming)

DAVE BRINKS
The Caveat Onus
The Secret Brain: Selected Poems 1995–2012

RUXANDRA CESEREANU
Crusader-Woman. Translated by Adam J. Sorkin.
    Introduction by Andrei Codrescu.
Forgiven Submarine by Ruxandra Cesereanu
    and Andrei Codrescu.

CLAYTON ESHLEMAN
An Alchemist with One Eye on Fire
Anticline
Archaic Design
Clayton Eshleman/The Essential Poetry: 1960–2015
Grindstone of Rapport: A Clayton Eshleman Reader
Penetralia
Pollen Aria
The Price of Experience
Endure: Poems by Bei Dao. Translated by
    Clayton Eshleman and Lucas Klein.
Curdled Skulls: Poems of Bernard Bador.
    Translated by Bernard Bador with
    Clayton Eshleman.

PIERRE JORIS
Barzakh (Poems 2000–2012)
Exile Is My Trade: A Habib Tengour Reader

MARILYN KALLET
Even When We Sleep
How Our Bodies Learned
Packing Light: New and Selected Poems
The Love That Moves Me
Disenchanted City (La ville désenchantée)
    by Chantal Bizzini. Translated by
    J. Bradford Anderson, Darren Jackson,
    and Marilyn Kallet.

ROBERT KELLY
Fire Exit
The Hexagon

STEPHEN KESSLER
Garage Elegies
Last Call

BILL LAVENDER
Memory Wing

HELLER LEVINSON
from stone this running
jus' sayn'
LinguaQuake
Lure
Lurk
Seep
Tenebraed
Un-
Wrack Lariat

JOHN OLSON
Backscatter: New and Selected Poems
Dada Budapest
Larynx Galaxy
Weave of the Dream King

NIYI OSUNDARE
City Without People: The Katrina Poems
Green: Sighs of Our Ailing Planet / Poems

MEBANE ROBERTSON
An American Unconscious
Signal from Draco: New and Selected Poems

JEROME ROTHENBERG
Concealments and Caprichos
Eye of Witness: A Jerome Rothenberg Reader.
    Edited with commentaries by Heriberto
    Yepez & Jerome Rothenberg.
The President of Desolation & Other Poems

AMINA SAÏD
The Present Tense of the World: Poems 2000–2009.
    Translated with an introduction by Marilyn Hacker.

ANIS SHIVANI
Soraya (Sonnets)

JERRY W. WARD, JR.
Fractal Song

BLACK WIDOW PRESS :: ANTHOLOGIES / BIOGRAPHIES

Barbaric Vast & Wild: A Gathering of Outside and Subterranean Poetry (Poems for the Millennium, vol. 5). Jerome Rothenberg and John Bloomberg-Rissman, editors.

Clayton Eshleman: The Whole Art by Stuart Kendall

Revolution of the Mind: The Life of André Breton by Mark Polizzotti